Collins

11+
English
Quick Practice Tests
Ages 9-10

Faisal Nasim

Contents

ACKNOWLEDGEMENTS

The author and publisher are grateful to the copyright holders for permission to use quoted materials and images.

p.14 The Cyclops, from *Heroes and Villains* by, Anthony Horowitz, © Anthony Horowitz 2011, published by Macmillan Books.

p.24 Excerpt from *WHERE THE RED FERN GROWS*, by Wilson Rawls, © 1961 by Sophie S. Rawls, Trustee or successor Trustee of the Rawls Trust, dated July 31st, 1991. © 1961 The Curtis Publishing Company. Used by permission of Delacorte Press, an imprint of Random House Children's Books, a division of Random House LLC. All rights reserved.

p.34 From: *Icons of England*, edited by Bill Bryson published by Black Swan. Reprinted by permission of the Random House Group Limited © 2010. Also © Telegraph Media Group Limited 2010 for the rights they hold.

p.44 Extract from: *Jack Russell Dog Breed*, taken from: Petwave Website. © Petwave. Used by permission of Petwave. For further reading, please visit http://www.petwave.com/Dogs/Breeds/Jack-Russell-Terrier.aspx

p.53 Birds and your Garden was taken from the Natural England Website and is used under the Open Government License.

Every effort has been made to trace copyright holders and obtain their permission for the use of copyright material. The author and publisher will gladly receive information enabling them to rectify any error or omission in subsequent editions. All facts are correct at time of going to press.

Published by Collins
An imprint of HarperCollins*Publishers* Limited
1 London Bridge Street, London SE1 9GF

HarperCollins*Publishers*
Macken House, 39/40 Mayor Street Upper, Dublin 1, D01 C9W8, Ireland

ISBN: 9781844199143

First published 2018; this edition 2020
Previously published by Letts

10 9

© HarperCollins*Publishers* Limited 2020

Author and Series Editor: Faisal Nasim
Commissioning Editor: Michelle I'Anson
Editor and Project Manager: Sonia Dawkins
Cover Design: Sarah Duxbury and Kevin Robbins
Text and Page Design: Ian Wrigley
Layout and Artwork: Q2A Media
Production: Natalia Rebow
Printed in India by Multivista Global Pvt. Ltd.

MIX
Paper | Supporting responsible forestry
FSC™ C007454

This book is produced from independently certified FSC™ paper to ensure responsible forest management.

For more information visit: www.harpercollins.co.uk/green

About this book

Familiarisation with 11+ test-style questions is a critical step in preparing your child for the 11+ selection tests. This book gives children lots of opportunities to test themselves in short, manageable bursts, helping to build confidence and improve the chance of test success.

It contains 29 tests designed to develop key English skills.

- Each test is designed to be completed within a short amount of time. Frequent, short bursts of revision are found to be more productive than lengthier sessions.

- GL Assessment tests can be quite time-pressured so these practice tests will help your child become accustomed to this style of questioning.

- We recommend your child uses a pencil to complete the tests, so that they can rub out the answers and try again at a later date if necessary.

- Children will need a pencil and a rubber to complete the tests as well as some spare paper for rough working. They will also need to be able to see a clock/watch and should have a quiet place in which to do the tests.

- Answers to every question are provided at the back of the book, with explanations given where appropriate.

- After completing the tests, children should revisit their weaker areas and attempt to improve their scores and timings.

Download a free progress chart from our website
collins.co.uk/11plus

Comprehension

You have 10 minutes to complete this test.

You have 10 questions to complete within the time given.

Read the passage and answer the questions that follow. In each question, circle the letter next to the correct answer.

EXAMPLE

Adam applauded the diver as she stepped onto the podium to collect her Olympic silver medal.

In which sport did the athlete compete?

A   Rowing

B   Gymnastics

C   Hockey

(D)   Diving

E   Football

The following is an extract from 'Black Beauty' by Anna Sewell

At this time I used to stand in the stable and my coat was brushed every day till it shone like a rook's wing. It was early in May, when there came a man from Squire Gordon's, who took me away to the hall. My master said, "Good-bye, Darkie; be a good horse, and always do your best." I could not say "good-bye", so I put my nose into his hand; he patted me kindly, and I left my first
5   home. As I lived some years with Squire Gordon, I may as well tell something about the place.

Squire Gordon's park skirted the village of Birtwick. It was entered by a large iron gate, at which stood the first lodge, and then you trotted along on a smooth road between clumps of large old trees; then another lodge and another gate, which brought you to the house and the gardens. Beyond this lay the home paddock, the old orchard, and the stables. There was
10   accommodation for many horses and carriages; but I need only describe the stable into which I was taken; this was very roomy, with four good stalls; a large swinging window opened into the yard, which made it pleasant and airy.

The first stall was a large square one, shut in behind with a wooden gate; the others were common stalls, good stalls, but not nearly so large; it had a low rack for hay and a low manger
15   for corn; it was called a loose box, because the horse that was put into it was not tied up, but left loose, to do as he liked. It is a great thing to have a loose box.

Into this fine box the groom put me; it was clean, sweet, and airy. I never was in a better box than that, and the sides were not so high but that I could see all that went on through the iron rails that were at the top.

20 He gave me some very nice oats, he patted me, spoke kindly, and then went away. When I had eaten my corn I looked round. In the stall next to mine stood a little fat gray horse, with a thick mane and tail, a very pretty head, and a pert little nose.

I put my head up to the iron rails at the top of my box, and said, "How do you do? What is your name?"

25 He turned round as far as his halter would allow, held up his head, and said, "My name is Merrylegs. I am very handsome; I carry the young ladies on my back, and sometimes I take our mistress out in the low chair. They think a great deal of me, and so does James. Are you going to live next door to me in the box?"

I said, "Yes."

30 "Well, then," he said, "I hope you are good-tempered; I do not like any one next door who bites."

Just then a horse's head looked over from the stall beyond; the ears were laid back, and the eye looked rather ill-tempered. This was a tall chestnut mare, with a long handsome neck. She looked across to me and said:

"So it is you who have turned me out of my box; it is a very strange thing for a colt like you to
35 come and turn a lady out of her own home."

---

(1) How many different horses are mentioned in this passage?

A   One

B   Two

C   Three

D   Four

E   None

(2) In which month do the events in this passage take place?

A   January

B   May

C   June

D   December

E   April

(3) What is the name of the horse's second master?

A   It is not mentioned in the passage.

B   Merrylegs

C   Squire Gordon

D   James

E   Black Beauty

Questions continue on next page

(4) Which of these statements best describes the stable?

A   It was very jammed and cluttered.

B   It was very spacious and airy.

C   It hardly had any air circulation.

D   It was very unpleasant.

E   It was hard and uncomfortable.

(5) What is a loose box?

A   It is a box used to transport horses from one estate to another.

B   It is a stall in which the horse is not tied up.

C   It refers to when the horse is allowed to roam free on the land.

D   It is a larger than average sized stall.

E   It is a stall that has no walls.

(6) Which of these statements is false?

A   One of the horses was very proud.

B   The stable had four stalls.

C   One of the horses was grey.

D   The groom was very kind to the new horse that came to the stable.

E   The horse was very happy to leave his first master and move to the new stable.

(7) How did Merrylegs look?

A   Pretty and plump, with a thick mane and tail

B   Ugly and thin

C   Unpleasant and underfed

D   Famished and skinny

E   Old, majestic and royal

(8) Why was the mare not very happy with the arrival of the new horse?

A   Because she had to vacate her stall to make room for the new horse.

B   Because she preferred to be alone.

C   Because she preferred the stall to remain empty.

D   Because she feared new competition.

E   Because she had a bad previous experience with a similar horse.

9 Which of these is an antonym of 'loose', as it is used in the passage? (line 16)

A   Tight

B   Gain

C   Tied

D   Slack

E   Sag

10 What type of words are these?

patted, brought, allow, was

A   Adjectives

B   Nouns

C   Adverbs

D   Verbs

E   Pronouns

Score: .... / 10

Test 2	# Spelling

You have 6 minutes to complete this test.

You have 12 questions to complete within the time given.

In each question, circle the letter below the group of words containing a spelling mistake.

If there is no mistake, circle the letter **N**.

EXAMPLE

The peeple at the festival enjoyed the party atmosphere as the moon rose high overhead.

(A)   B   C   D   **N**

---

(1) Charlotte had always been considered as a dependeble member of the team.

A   B   C   D   **N**

(2) Neither of my asistants was able to solve the case so I will need to get involved.

A   B   C   D   **N**

(3) Salford City are a good football team, at least acording to him.

A   B   C   D   **N**

(4) "I seek the coperation of all those affected," declared the politician magnanimously.

A   B   C   D   **N**

(5) The obedient hound was rewarded with a juicy pork chop, which she devoured instantly.

A   B   C   D   **N**

(6) The horrendous criminal showed not even a shred of remorse or decensy at the trial.

A   B   C   D   **N**

8

(7) Sales of stationary tend to spike just prior to the beginning of the new school year.

    A   B   C   D   [N]

(8) Both patience and gratitude are esential and required traits if you want to work here.

    A   B   C   D   [N]

(9) Rebecca was impressed by the young student's self-confidence and assuredness.

    A   B   C   D   [N]

(10) A slimy green substance oozed out of the vile and dripped slowly down on to the floor.

    A   B   C   D   [N]

(11) The robber managed to steel my bag when my attention had been diverted elsewhere.

    A   B   C   D   [N]

(12) The engineer felt relieved after he transfered all his savings to his new bank account.

    A   B   C   D   [N]

You have 6 minutes to complete this test.

You have 12 questions to complete within the time given.

In each question, circle the letter below the group of words containing a punctuation mistake.

If there is no mistake, circle the letter **N**.

EXAMPLE

The fireworks reflected in the thames to produce a brilliant and colourful display.

    A   (B)   C   D   **N**

---

1 I like Paris and New York, but london is my favourite city; I love playing in all the parks.

    A   B   C   D   **N**

2 Her sister was unable to join the others as she had developed a stomach infection

    A   B   C   D   **N**

3 Very few of the survivors had received adequate support from the authorities.

    A   B   C   D   **N**

4 Ben James and Carl all wanted to visit the new exhibition when it opened in November.

    A   B   C   D   **N**

5 "Where are we going," asked Jenny as she stared out of the window in bewilderment.

    A   B   C   D   **N**

6 There isnt a single painting in this pretentious art gallery that I would hang on my walls.

    A   B   C   D   **N**

(7) The hospitals' most senior doctors discussed the possible causes of the mystery illnesses.

     A   B   C   D   N

(8) The giraffe wished to eat the succulent tree shrubs. However she was not tall enough.

     A   B   C   D   N

(9) Here is a list of ingredients: Butter, eggs, milk, baking soda, cocoa, flour and sugar.

     A   B   C   D   N

(10) The rain poured for hours without pause; Many buildings were damaged by flooding.

     A   B   C   D   N

(11) The hungry traveller ordered meat, and potatoes as a main course at the restaurant.

     A   B   C   D   N

(12) Ellen and Jane got along well although Jane frequently argued with Ellen's friend, rebecca.

     A   B   C   D   N

Test	# Sentence Completion
4	You have 6 minutes to complete this test. You have 12 questions to complete within the time given.

In each question, circle the letter below the word or group of words that most accurately completes the passage.

EXAMPLE

Finding a replacement | **change** | **chart** | **chance** | **charge** | **charger** | for her phone wasn't easy.
                                         A   B   C   Ⓓ   E

① "Can you see those two boys over there? This ball belongs to | **hers** | **it** | **them** | **their** | **his** |,"
                                                                      A   B   C   D   E

said Emma.

② All of the competitors will run | **past** | **together** | **passed** | **between** | **either** | this green
                                        A   B   C   D   E

flag on the way to the finish line.

③ Robert placed the bouquet of flowers | **in** | **with** | **at** | **from** | **pole** | the foot of the
                                              A   B   C   D   E

monument.

④ Tim ate a | **hole** | **entire** | **empty** | **thirsty** | **whole** | pack of cookies before lunch and so
                        A   B   C   D   E

he was not hungry.

⑤ | **Moreover** | **Because** | **Despite** | **Indeed** | **Furthermore** | the setback, Fraser
      A   B   C   D   E

managed to complete the task successfully.

(6) Nobody | **would of** | | **can** | | **can't have** | | **could have** | | **could of** | predicted that the game
        A   **B**   **C**   **D**   **E**

would end in such a dramatic fashion.

(7) Veronica, | **whom** | | **who** | | **whose** | | **who's** | | **who'd** | preferred to be called Vera, made her
           A   **B**   **C**   **D**   **E**

way to the stage to speak.

(8) "| **Still** | | **Stay** | | **Staying** | | **Stayed** | | **Be stay** | there!" ordered my mother as she ran to
     A   **B**   **C**   **D**   **E**

the counter to seek help.

(9) The rocket blasted | **with** | | **in** | | **through** | | **on** | | **for** | the earth's atmosphere into space.
                    A   **B**   **C**   **D**   **E**

(10) "What would you like to | **be** | | **is** | | **being** | | **was** | | **were** | when you grow up?" asked
                          A   **B**   **C**   **D**   **E**

my teacher.

(11) Wendy's favourite colour is red. | **Therefore** | | **As such** | | **However** | | **Thus** | | **So** |, she also
                                   A   **B**   **C**   **D**   **E**

likes blue.

(12) David | **was went** | | **has been going** | | **has went** | | **had went** | | **had been gone** | to the
         A   **B**   **C**   **D**   **E**

same gym for over fifteen years.

Test	# Comprehension
5	You have 10 minutes to complete this test. You have 10 questions to complete within the time given.

Read the passage and answer the questions that follow. In each question, circle the letter next to the correct answer.

EXAMPLE

Adam applauded the diver as she stepped onto the podium to collect her Olympic silver medal.

In which sport did the athlete compete?

A Rowing

B Gymnastics

C Hockey

(D) Diving

E Football

The following is an extract from 'Heroes and Villains' by Anthony Horowitz

The Cyclops was certainly a terrifying creature. It was about the height of a two-storey house with thick, curly hair, a matted (and usually filthy) beard and only one eye, set square in the middle of its forehead. It was grotesquely ugly, extremely bad-tempered, inordinately violent and generally worth going a long way to avoid. All this, any good book of Greek myths will tell
5 you. But what is less often mentioned is the fact that the Cyclops was also incredibly stupid. It was probably one of the most stupid monsters that ever lived.

There were a great many Cyclopes. At one time they had been employed as blacksmiths for Zeus but after a while they had forgotten not only how to do the work but what the work was that they were supposed to do, and had become shepherds instead. They were shepherds for almost
10 two hundred years before it occurred to them to go and buy some sheep. Then they took their sheep and settled on an island in the middle of the Aegean Sea where they lived in caves, seldom if ever talking to one another. There were two reasons for this. The first was that the Cyclopes were poor conversationalists, often forgetting the beginning of a sentence when they were only halfway through. But also, if there was one thing a Cyclops couldn't stand, it was another Cyclops.

15 The most famous Cyclops was called Polyphemus. He was the son of Poseidon, the god of the sea, but preferred to stay very much on land, looking after a flock of sheep. Polyphemus had no friends but was on intimate terms with most of the sheep. He knew them all by name, chatted to them, milked them as gently as his huge fingers could manage and shed real tears whenever he had to slaughter one in order to make his particularly delicious lamb stew.

20 One day, returning to his cave after a hard day's work in the hills, he was astonished to find that he had visitors. They were still there in fact, sitting in front of his fire and feasting on one of his

sheep. There were about a dozen of them and, looking more closely, he was delighted to see that they were human beings.

Polyphemus loved human beings in his own way… which was cooked or raw. What he particularly
25 liked about them was the way their bones crunched between his teeth but never got caught in his throat.

The giant's face lit up in a great smile. It was also a horrible smile for having just one eye in the middle of his face, everything he did with his face was rather horrible.

'Who are you?' he demanded.

30 The men had by now huddled together and were looking up at him with a mixture of horror and terror. Then one of them stepped forward.

'Good monster,' he said, 'we are Greeks. We are returning home, having fought a great war at Troy. We stopped here to find fresh provisions for our ship and thought to pass the night in your cave.'

35 Polyphemus scowled. He had never heard of Troy and didn't particularly like being addressed as 'monster'.

The man bowed low. 'I am sure you need no reminding,' he said, 'of the laws of Zeus, which demand hospitality to poor travellers such as ourselves. And I…'

But he was wasting his time. Polyphemus didn't even know what 'hospitality' meant. Moreover,
40 he was hungry.

---

(1) Which of these was the safest strategy to pursue upon encountering a Cyclops?

    A   Make friends with the Cyclops

    B   Grin at the Cyclops

    C   Avoid the Cyclops

    D   Kill the Cyclops

    E   Spend a day with the Cyclops

(2) Which of the following statements is true?

    A   Cyclopes had an outstanding memory.

    B   Zeus employed them as gardeners.

    C   Cyclopes were excellent blacksmiths.

    D   Cyclopes were incredibly dim-witted.

    E   Cyclopes lived in the Atlantic Ocean.

Questions continue on next page

(3) Why were Cyclopes poor communicators?

    A   They had big teeth that prevented them from speaking.

    B   Their memory and understanding were poor.

    C   They had better things to do than to communicate.

    D   They were more interested in rearing their sheep.

    E   They hardly had any time to communicate.

(4) Which of the following best describes Polyphemus' relationship with his sheep?

    A   He was distant and formal with them.

    B   He was cruel to them.

    C   He hardly took any interest in them.

    D   He was totally indifferent to them.

    E   He cherished his close relationship with them.

(5) Where did Polyphemus live?

    A   In a cave

    B   In a tree

    C   In a ship

    D   Between haystacks

    E   In a fortress

(6) What was Polyphemus' reaction to realising there were humans in his home?

    A   He was disgusted.

    B   He was overjoyed.

    C   He was distraught.

    D   He was furious.

    E   He was nonchalant.

(7) How did the men react to seeing Polyphemus?

    A   The men gathered together in fright.

    B   The men ran away as fast as they could.

    C   The men refused to talk to Polyphemus.

    D   The men were afraid to even enter his cave.

    E   The men huddled together in joy.

(8) Why were the men on the island?

    A   The men were soldiers looking to conquer the island.

    B   The men were sent by Apollo to meet Polyphemus.

    C   The men had got lost and landed on the island by mistake.

    D   The men were in search of food and water.

    E   The men had come to kill Polyphemus.

(9) Which of these is a synonym of 'hospitality'? (line 39)

    A   Generosity

    B   Hospitals

    C   Injury

    D   Prejudice

    E   Hopefulness

(10) Which of these is an antonym of 'violent'? (line 3)

    A   Strong

    B   Fierce

    C   Calmness

    D   Peaceful

    E   Cruel

Score: .... / 10

Spelling

In each question, circle the letter below the group of words containing a spelling mistake.

If there is no mistake, circle the letter **N**.

EXAMPLE

The peeple at the festival enjoyed the party atmosphere as the moon rose high overhead.

(A)   B   C   D   N

(1) Half of the climers are still stranded and it's unlikely that they will be rescued today.

A   B   C   D   N

(2) The support that she received from her local community was nothing short of incredable.

A   B   C   D   N

(3) The demolition process was only partially completed so half the flats remained in place.

A   B   C   D   N

(4) Farmers in New Zealand rear an extreemely large proportion of the world's lambs.

A   B   C   D   N

(5) There was only one guessed who arrived late; luckily, all the others arrived punctually.

A   B   C   D   N

(6) The young doctor dreamed of the day she would finally be able to open her own practise.

A   B   C   D   N

(7) Darren was anxious to proceed but the right ocasion had not yet presented itself.

A   B   C   D   N

(8) Mr Smith was known as an agreaable and amiable fellow, much beloved by his family.

A   B   C   D   N

(9) The diligent accountant maintained a ledjer of all the company's transactions.

A   B   C   D   N

(10) The camel wondered through the desert until night fell and it paused to take a rest.

A   B   C   D   N

(11) Finn took a deep breathe and then plunged headfirst into the freezing lake.

A   B   C   D   N

(12) My wife and I like to exercize early in the morning, before eating breakfast.

A   B   C   D   N

Score: .... / 12

19

Punctuation

In each question, circle the letter below the group of words containing a punctuation mistake.

If there is no mistake, circle the letter **N**.

EXAMPLE

The fireworks reflected in the thames to produce a brilliant and colourful display.

A   (B)   C   D   **N**

---

① "How could you do that!" demanded Sandra incredulously. "You've ruined everything!"

A   B   C   D   **N**

② Fishing requires skill, patience, good timing and, of course a little bit of luck!

A   B   C   D   **N**

③ Zaynab didn't submit her paper before the deadline. Nevertheless we accepted it.

A   B   C   D   **N**

④ The foreman, who fiercely protected the rights of his workers, began to prepare his case.

A   B   C   D   **N**

⑤ Patrick was excitedly looking forward to watching his favourite film; Star Wars.

A   B   C   D   **N**

⑥ The cricket pitch lies North of the school, around 200 metres from the supermarket.

A   B   C   D   **N**

(7) There werent enough chairs for everyone to sit as the room was absolutely packed.

     A   B   C   D   N

(8) There's a great fish restaurant there called the Codfather. I'd definitely recommend it.

     A   B   C   D   N

(9) "We wouldn't want anyone to come to any harm." snickered the wicked headmaster.

     A   B   C   D   N

(10) There were plans to build twenty-five new schools in the district over the next decade

     A   B   C   D   N

(11) The margherita pizza – or what was left of it – was quickly devoured by the hungry dog.

     A   B   C   D   N

(12) Pushing past the oblivious shoppers Vikki activated the alarm before it was too late.

     A   B   C   D   N

Score: .... / 12

Sentence Completion

In each question, circle the letter below the word or group of words that most accurately completes the passage.

EXAMPLE

Finding a replacement | **change** | **chart** | **chance** | **charge** | **charger** | for her phone wasn't easy.
　　　　　　　　　　　　　　A　　　　　B　　　　　C　　　　　Ⓓ　　　　　E

1. "That car belongs | **up** | **to** | **on** | **with** | **from** | my father," said the proud young man.
　　　　　　　　　　　　A　　B　　C　　D　　E

2. | **They'res** | **There's** | **Theirs** | **They're** | **Theres** | very little to do in this town in the
　　A　　　　　　B　　　　　　C　　　　　D　　　　　E

   evening. It's quite sleepy here.

3. Each of the club's members | **has** | **was** | **have** | **were** | **having** | given a personalised pen
　　　　　　　　　　　　　　　　A　　　　B　　　　C　　　　D　　　　E

   upon completing their first month.

4. Tina's pile of buttons was | **comparisons** | **company** | **comparing** | **comparatively** |
　　　　　　　　　　　　　　　　A　　　　　　　　B　　　　　　C　　　　　　D

   | **comparison** | small.
　　　E

5. Based | **on** | **with** | **from** | **up** | **for** | her performance last year, the snowboarder was
　　　　　A　　B　　　C　　　D　　E

   considered the favourite.

6   "It's good that | your | youre | yore | yours | you're | here," said my mother happily.
                           A   B   C   D   E

7   "Given | up | due | that | since | for | you have no relevant experience, I can't possibly
            A   B   C   D   E

offer you a job."

8   Kim jumped | under | with | over | directly | away | the pile of leaves on the ground and
                  A   B   C   D   E

landed on the soft grass.

9   Even though it was dark, I could still | flow | see | hope | sea | hear | the time shown on
                                    A   B   C   D   E

the clock.

10   The teacher clearly disapproved | because | with | on | of | in | the unruly student's
                               A   B   C   D   E

behaviour.

11   The beautiful dog took a number of months to recover | in | by | form | off | from | her
                                          A   B   C   D   E

injuries.

12   They didn't | needing | needed | needer | needs | need | to be reminded of how
                  A   B   C   D   E

important the event was.

Score: .... / 12

Read the passage and answer the questions that follow. In each question, circle the letter next to the correct answer.

EXAMPLE

Adam applauded the diver as she stepped onto the podium to collect her Olympic silver medal.

In which sport did the athlete compete?

A   Rowing

B   Gymnastics

C   Hockey

(D)   Diving

E   Football

The following is an extract from 'Where the Red Fern Grows' by Wilson Rawls

When I left my office that beautiful spring day, I had no idea what was in store for me. To begin with, everything was too perfect for anything unusual to happen. It was one of those days when a man feels good, feels like speaking to his neighbour, is glad to live in a country like ours. You know what I mean, one of those rare days when everything is right and nothing is wrong. I was
5   walking along whistling when I heard the dogfight. At first I paid no attention to it. After all it wasn't anything to get excited about, just another dogfight in a residential section.

As the sound of the fight grew nearer, I could tell there were quite a few dogs mixed up in it. They boiled out of an alley, turned, and headed straight toward me. Not wanting to get bitten or run over, I moved over to the edge of the sidewalk. I could see that all the dogs were fighting
10   one. About twenty-five feet from me they caught him and down he went. I felt sorry for the unfortunate one. I knew if something wasn't done quickly the sanitation department would have to pick up a dead dog. I was trying to make up my mind to help when I got a surprise. Up out of that snarling, growling, slashing mass reared an old redbone hound. For a second I saw him. I caught my breath. I couldn't believe what I had seen.

15   Twisting and slashing, he fought his way through the pack and backed up under the low branches of a hedge. Growling and snarling, they formed a half-moon circle around him. A big bird dog, bolder than the others, darted in. The hedge shook as he tangled with the hound. He came out so fast he fell over backwards. I saw that his right ear was split wide open. It was too much for him and he took off down the street, squalling like a scalded cat. A big ugly dog tried
20   his luck. He didn't get off so easy. He came out with his left shoulder laid open to the bone. He

sat down on his rear and let the world know that he had been hurt. By this time, my fighting
blood was boiling. It's hard for a man to stand and watch an old hound fight against such odds,
especially if that man has memories in his heart like I had in mine. I had seen the time when
an old hound like that had given his life so that I might live. Taking off my coat, I waded in. My
25 yelling and scolding didn't have much effect, but the swinging coat did. The dogs scattered and
left. Down on my knees, I peered back under the hedge. The hound was still mad. He growled
at me and showed his teeth. I knew it wasn't his nature to fight a man. In a soft voice, I started
talking to him. "Come on, boy," I said. "It's all right. I'm your friend. Come on now." The fighting
fire slowly left his eyes. He bowed his head and his long, red tail started thumping the ground.
30 I kept coaxing. On his stomach, an inch at a time, he came to me and laid his head in my hand.
I almost cried at what I saw. His coat was dirty and mud-caked. His skin was stretched drum-
tight over his bony frame. The knotty joints of his hips and shoulders stood out a good three
inches from his body. I could tell he was starved. I couldn't figure it out. He didn't belong in
town. He was far out of place with the boxers, poodles, bird dogs, and other breeds of town
35 dogs. He belonged in the country. He was a hunting hound.

I raised one of his paws. There I read the story. The pads were worn down slick as the rind on an
apple. I knew he had come a long way, and no doubt had a long way to go. Around his neck was
a crude collar. On closer inspection, I saw it had been made from a piece of check-line leather.
Two holes had been punched in each end and the ends were laced together with bailing wire. As I
40 turned the collar with my finger, I saw something else. There, scratched deep in the tough leather,
was the name "Buddie". I guessed that the crude, scribbly letters had probably been written by a
little boy.

① In which month could the events in this passage have taken place?

A   December

B   July

C   April

D   January

E   August

② How was the narrator's mood before he witnessed the dogfight?

A   He was extremely tense and anxious.

B   He was exhausted from the day's events.

C   He was relaxed and content.

D   He was worried about the evening to come.

E   He was melancholic.

Questions continue on next page

3 What happened if a deceased dog was found on the streets?

    A   It would be fed to scavengers.

    B   It would be cleared by the sanitation department.

    C   It would be left to rot.

    D   It would be thrown into the playground.

    E   Nobody would bother about it.

4 '…an old hound like that had given his life so that I might live.' (line 24)

What conclusion can be drawn from this line?

    A   The narrator had been saved by a dog.

    B   The narrator hated dogs.

    C   The narrator was scared of dogs.

    D   The narrator had once saved a dog's life.

    E   The narrator was fond of all dogs.

5 How did the narrator finally disperse the attacking dogs?

    A   He swung his coat at them.

    B   He yelled and shouted at them.

    C   He threw stones at them.

    D   He called the police.

    E   He attacked them with his bare hands.

6 How did the hound dog react to the narrator?

    A   The hound was at first welcoming and then turned aggressive.

    B   The hound reacted violently.

    C   The hound was at first joyful and then turned ambivalent.

    D   The hound reacted negatively.

    E   The hound was at first on guard but then approached the man.

7 Which of these quotes from the passage indicate that the old hound was famished?

    A   His coat was dirty and mud-caked.

    B   He belonged in the country.

    C   He was a hunting hound.

    D   The fighting fire slowly left his eyes.

    E   His skin was stretched drum-tight over his bony frame.

8 Which of these statements is false?

    A   The paws of the dog were worn out.

    B   Hounds generally don't fight men.

    C   The narrator was trying to help the old hound.

    D   The old hound belonged to the local neighbourhood.

    E   Many dogs attacked the old hound.

9 'I caught my breath.' (line 13–14)

What does this sentence mean?

    A   The narrator was hungry.

    B   The narrator had to hold still.

    C   The narrator was surprised.

    D   The narrator was ill.

    E   The narrator had a headache.

10 Which of these is a synonym of 'inspection'? (line 38)

    A   Inspector

    B   Maintenance

    C   Rite

    D   Ceremony

    E   Examination

Score: .... / 10

Spelling

You have 6 minutes to complete this test.

You have 12 questions to complete within the time given.

In each question, circle the letter below the group of words containing a spelling mistake.

If there is no mistake, circle the letter **N**.

EXAMPLE

The peeple at the festival enjoyed the party atmosphere as the moon rose high overhead.
  (A)   B   C   D | N |

---

1. The hotel operated at maximum capasity throughout the busy summer months.
   A   B   C   D | N |

2. There were many arguements in the noisy street below, so Joel found it difficult to sleep.
   A   B   C   D | N |

3. The instructor aught not to have allowed the novice to fly the plane without supervision.
   A   B   C   D | N |

4. Few realised at the time how disastrous the affects would be for the local region.
   A   B   C   D | N |

5. Animals that exclusively eat plants and vegetables are known as herbivores.
   A   B   C   D | N |

6. The powerful foreign states convened at the sponference to discuss international affairs.
   A   B   C   D | N |

(7) The deceased pensioner was berried in the cemetery beside the local church.

    A   B   C   D   **N**

(8) Diana wanted to go shopping to buy a cubboard for her room in the new house.

    A   B   C   D   **N**

(9) Cleaning material and chemicals can be found in the third isle of the supermarket.

    A   B   C   D   **N**

(10) The remarkable John Logie Baird was one of the inventers of the television.

    A   B   C   D   **N**

(11) Jillian was a Londoner born and bread, and loved to show off her city to newcomers.

    A   B   C   D   **N**

(12) The appartment was not furnished, yet it was still more expensive than the others.

    A   B   C   D   **N**

Score: .... / 12

Punctuation

In each question, circle the letter below the group of words containing a punctuation mistake.

If there is no mistake, circle the letter **N**.

EXAMPLE

The fireworks reflected in the thames to produce a brilliant and colourful display.

A   **Ⓑ**   C   D   **N**

---

(1) Ben's newest car's brake light's were especially bright and visible at night.

A   B   C   D   **N**

(2) What is the meaning of life. Come to our class this afternoon to find out for yourself.

A   B   C   D   **N**

(3) The dragon reared its heavy head and began to snort puffs of smoke from it's nostrils.

A   B   C   D   **N**

(4) They were only a few days into Autumn but the temperature was already plunging.

A   B   C   D   **N**

(5) "This frisbee is theirs," stated my father as he tossed it to our neighbour over the fence.

A   B   C   D   **N**

(6) "The three things you need for a perfect holiday are sun, sea and, sand," she said.

A   B   C   D   **N**

(7) When the gigantic clock struck seven the bell rang exactly seven times.

    A   B   C   D   **N**

(8) We hope to leave for Spain next thursday and then don't plan to return until mid-July.

    A   B   C   D   **N**

(9) "The game will begin in one hour," declared the referee. Please ensure you are ready."

    A   B   C   D   **N**

(10) The flight will leave from Heathrow Airport (Terminal 2) in exactly 45 minutes.

    A   B   C   D   **N**

(11) Several sources claim that the accused could not have been at the scene at two oclock.

    A   B   C   D   **N**

(12) William was in a mood to argue. Unwilling to start a fight Daisy decided to keep quiet.

    A   B   C   D   **N**

Test 12	**Sentence Completion**
	You have 6 minutes to complete this test.
	You have 12 questions to complete within the time given.

In each question, circle the letter below the word or group of words that most accurately completes the passage.

EXAMPLE

Finding a replacement | change | chart | chance | charge | charger | for her phone wasn't easy.
              A   B   C   D   (E)

---

(1) Ian couldn't wait to go to the zoo and see all the | hoses | papers | ticks | animals |
               A   B   C   D

| corners |.
  E

(2) Last week, the woman | eats | eat | ate | ated | is eating | a sandwich over there by
          A   B   C   D   E

the river.

(3) The legal firm specialised | on | above | with | in | for | corporate and public law.
          A   B   C   D   E

(4) The eagle, | which | whose | those | that's | witch | had been circling for hours, zoomed
          A   B   C   D   E

down and caught the mouse.

(5) None of the participants | where | was | were | is | isn't | able to make it through to the
          A   B   C   D   E

next round.

6. The old lady lost [his] [her] [hers] [theirs] [it's] glasses and so she could not see properly.
                  A   **B**   **C**   **D**   **E**

7. There are more men [then] [of] [as] [than] [over] women at this party.
                  A   **B** **C**   **D**   **E**

8. The hungry fox [safe] [sudden] [quickly] [quick] [lowly] devoured the tasty morsel in
               A   **B**   **C**   **D**   **E**

the garden.

9. Beth stretched her hands up as high [of] [in] [with] [from] [as] she could manage.
                               A **B**   **C**   **D**   **E**

10. "[Don't] [Didn't] [Dont] [Doesn't] [Does] worry about it," reassured the manager.
     A   **B**   **C**   **D**   **E**

11. "[Got] [Gets] [Getter] [Get] [Getting] down!" cried the soldier as the bullets began to
     A   **B**   **C**   **D**   **E**

whistle past them.

12. Many of the attendees were keen to invest [for] [through] [in] [on] [over] the
                                          A   **B**   **C** **D**   **E**

new project.

Score: .... / 12

Test 13	# Comprehension
	You have 10 minutes to complete this test.
	You have 10 questions to complete within the time given.

Read the passage and answer the questions that follow. In each question, circle the letter next to the correct answer.

EXAMPLE

Adam applauded the diver as she stepped onto the podium to collect her Olympic silver medal.

In which sport did the athlete compete?

A   Rowing

B   Gymnastics

C   Hockey

(D)   Diving

E   Football

The following is an extract from 'Icons of England' edited by Bill Bryson

What greater icon could we have than our countryside, which I have always believed helps to define our identity as a nation? England is blessed with some of the most beautiful scenery in the world. The patchwork quilt of fields, moors, forests, villages, and market towns which spreads across this land is the product of a golden combination of Nature's gift to us and the toil and
5   care of generations of farmers and their families who have managed the land.

We shape and change the land. But if we want parts of it to stay the same, it's a subject that needs to be discussed. You can't just drive through it and leave it to chance. You've got to care about it. This article is an endeavour to change the attitude of people towards the countryside.

Sheltered from the brief spring squall by the high banks on either side of me, I walk briskly to
10   keep warm. Above me, clouds scud swiftly, framed by the bare branches of overhanging trees; seagulls, buffeted inland by the storm, slip sideways in the wind.

A gateway on my right draws me from the road. I lean on the top bar and survey the ploughed field. Newly turned soil lies glistening in long furrows – the rich red clay of south Devon. This country lane was the scene of Sunday strolls during my childhood when, every week, we had to
15   "walk our Sunday lunch down".

Fifty years on, instead of my brother and parents, I am accompanied by a walking stick. But the lane remains unchanged. Goose grass still grows along the hedgerow bottom. Just the same that I used to pick and plant on my brother's back.

The lane climbs gently upwards. The road has dried in the breeze, but the base of the bank is
20 damp. It is always damp. It's where the ferns flourish and the grass is lush, where dog violets
hide shyly in early spring and where frogs can be found.

The deep lanes of Devon remain untroubled by traffic. Fortunately drivers prefer the speedy
routes via motorway or trunk road. Apart from the distant tractor sound, it's birdsong, not
traffic noise, that keeps me company.

25 There are treasures in a Devon hedgerow. Obvious ones like wildflowers, and hidden ones, like
birds' nests or a basking lizard. I think of the flowers as stars. Vivid yellow stars are the first to
appear – celandines, followed later by the pure white star-like stitchwort. The stars of summer
are pink – roses, campion and herb robert – while autumn twinkles with bramble blossom. It
shines out in palest pink and white among the tangle of other hedgerow plants.

30 In summer, the heady scent of honeysuckle adds even more enjoyment to a walk along a Devon
lane, while autumn offers a harvest of elderberries, sloes, nuts and blackberries.

I reach another gap in the bank. From the open gateway I have a view across rolling hills down
to the Exe valley. The river is a silver ribbon; beside it parallel silver threads show the route of
the railway that follows the river until it reaches the mainline station of Exeter St David's.

35 But Exeter is only a faint smudge in the far distance and here, in the beautiful Devon
countryside, I am cocooned from it.

The lane continues to climb until it reaches Stoke Woods. These wooded heights are the site of
a Roman signal tower and, earlier still, a fortified tribal encampment. It's here that I stop and,
like my forebears, I soak up the tranquillity of a Devon lane – the ultimate rural icon.

---

(1) What is the purpose of this article?

    A   To belittle the English countryside.

    B   To change the reader's outlook towards cities.

    C   To change the reader's outlook towards the countryside.

    D   To discuss the English weather.

    E   To discuss the future of British industries.

(2) Why have the seagulls flown inland?

    A   They are searching for food inland.

    B   Storms have driven them inland.

    C   Predators have drawn them inland.

    D   They fly inland to build nests.

    E   They fly inland to find a mate.

Questions continue on next page

(3) What has happened to the country lane that the author frequented as a child?

    A   It has changed tremendously but is still recognisable.

    B   It has remained the same.

    C   A new paving has been built upon the lane.

    D   The same vegetation is present but the lane itself is different.

    E   Nature has altered the look and feel of the country lane.

(4) What is the ideal terrain for ferns to prosper?

    A   A dry and arid expanse of land

    B   Hard rocky patches

    C   Parched meadows with thick vegetation

    D   Barren woodlands

    E   Wet and soggy land

(5) Which of the following can be found in a Devon hedgerow?

    A   Alligators

    B   Snakes

    C   Birds' nests

    D   Hidden treasure chests

    E   Old coins

(6) What runs parallel to the railway lines?

    A   The motorway

    B   The river

    C   The vast fields

    D   The moors

    E   The coast of Devon

(7) 'I am cocooned from it.' (line 36)

What does this phrase mean?

    A   The author is shielded from urban life by the countryside.

    B   The author is insulated from the countryside.

    C   The author is exposed to urban life because she is in the countryside.

    D   The author has ambivalent feelings towards the countryside.

    E   The author enjoys observing butterflies.

(8) What does the author believe to be the greatest symbol of rural England?

   A   Stoke Woods

   B   Exeter railway station

   C   The Roman signal tower

   D   The country lane

   E   The beach

(9) 'The river is a silver ribbon' (line 33)

   What literary technique is used in this phrase?

   A   Simile

   B   Metaphor

   C   Exaggeration

   D   Idiom

   E   Proverb

(10) What type of word is 'tranquillity'? (line 39)

   A   Adverb

   B   Verb

   C   Participle

   D   Noun

   E   Adjective

Score: .... / 10

Test	# Spelling
14	You have 6 minutes to complete this test.
	You have 12 questions to complete within the time given.

In each question, circle the letter below the group of words containing a spelling mistake.

If there is no mistake, circle the letter **N**.

EXAMPLE

The peeple at the festival enjoyed the party atmosphere as the moon rose high overhead.

Ⓐ   B   C   D   N

---

(1) The architect survayed the building site where she hoped to design the new house.

A   B   C   D   N

(2) Hiking boots need to be strong and stirdy to withstand the effects of all terrains.

A   B   C   D   N

(3) The baker woke up early each morning to prepare the doe needed for his pastries.

A   B   C   D   N

(4) The perceived slight infuriated both the teacher and her teenage pupils.

A   B   C   D   N

(5) The organisers hoped the event would have a relaxed and friendly atmosfear.

A   B   C   D   N

(6) Henry marvelled at the gigantic galactic instalations and displays in the Science Museum.

A   B   C   D   N

(7) Billy was shocked to find a pear of starling chicks nesting under his bedroom window.

A   B   C   D   N

(8) The labourer toiled under the hot sun and was greateful when it began to rain.

A   B   C   D   N

(9) "A good secetary is difficult to find," stated Clare as she continued her search online.

A   B   C   D   N

(10) The tennis player refused to except the umpire's decision so he was penalised.

A   B   C   D   N

(11) The young actors and actresses were eagar to take part in their first production.

A   B   C   D   N

(12) The protesters were campaigning against the unfare treatment of the refugees.

A   B   C   D   N

Score: .... / 12

In each question, circle the letter below the group of words containing a punctuation mistake.

If there is no mistake, circle the letter **N**.

EXAMPLE

The fireworks reflected in the thames to produce a brilliant and colourful display.

     A   **(B)**   C   D   **N**

---

(1) "Whats the difference between these two designs?" asked Laura whilst browsing online.

     A   B   C   D   **N**

(2) The aquarium was filled with fish tuna, salmon, barracuda, cod, swordfish and sea bass.

     A   B   C   D   **N**

(3) It's unlikely we will find the puppy's owner as it's been a while and it's collar is missing.

     A   B   C   D   **N**

(4) "I can't concentrate on my revision with all this commotion!" Wailed Greg to his mother.

     A   B   C   D   **N**

(5) The removal men first attempted to carry the ugly heavy sofa down the stairs to the van.

     A   B   C   D   **N**

(6) Liverpool Street station is one of the largest and busiest transport hubs in London.

     A   B   C   D   **N**

(7) The young elephant loved to play in the grass follow his mother and splash in the lake.

    A   B   C   D   N

(8) "I broke my leg last week whilst playing football," said Jonathan. "I hope it heals soon".

    A   B   C   D   N

(9) The men's keys, watches and wallets were confiscated by the police at the scene.

    A   B   C   D   N

(10) Emma was delighted to receive the present she had been dreaming about – a puppy!

    A   B   C   D   N

(11) The journey from Aberdeen to Manchester is rather long and busy with traffic.

    A   B   C   D   N

(12) Tina was looking forward to spending a Bank holiday with her friends and family.

    A   B   C   D   N

Score: .... / 12

Sentence Completion

In each question, circle the letter below the word or group of words that most accurately completes the passage.

EXAMPLE

Finding a replacement | **change** | **chart** | **chance** | **charge** | **charger** | for her phone wasn't easy.
A   B   C   D   (E)

(1) Many of these species will | **beckon** | **become** | **became** | **becoming** | **becomes** |
     A   B   C   D   E

extinct within the next decade.

(2) The potent mixture was composed | **in** | **for** | **of** | **by** | **through** | water and acid.
     A   B   C   D   E

(3) To add insult | **to** | **in** | **above** | **through** | **from** | injury, the team were not only banned
     A   B   C   D   E

but also fined a substantial amount.

(4) You | **are being failed** | **have failed** | **have failing** | **are failed** | **have been failed** |
        A   B   C   D   E

to demonstrate why you should receive the funding.

(5) | **Withstanding** | **Whenever** | **Whoever** | **Whichever** | **Whatsoever** | path you
     A   B   C   D   E

choose, there will be significant obstacles along the way.

6 The cable broke as it was not | **weak** | **strong** | **line** | **rich** | **slow** | enough to hold their

                                                  A   B   C   D   E

combined weight.

7 I don't eat meat. | **Despite** | **Apart** | **Furthermore** | **However** | **Moreover** |, I am

                                     A   B   C   D   E

willing to make an exception on this occasion.

8 My mother used to say, "Don't | **pound** | **put** | **pretend** | **pressure** | **poke** | all your eggs

                                         A   B   C   D   E

in one basket."

9 There were no oranges left | **for** | **in** | **lest** | **before** | **so** | I bought some mangoes instead.

                                    A   B   C   D   E

10 | **Wherein** | **Wherever** | **Withhold** | **Witness** | **Whereas** | Jenny completed the

       A   B   C   D   E

assignment, James did not even begin it.

11 The sloth | **lazily** | **lazy** | **lazedly** | **lazed** | **laziness** | made its way across the

                      A   B   C   D   E

tree's branch.

12 The gigantic rocket blasted | **of** | **in** | **below** | **by** | **off** | into the sky just after midnight.

                                         A B   C   D   E

Score: / 12

Comprehension

Read the passage and answer the questions that follow. In each question, circle the letter next to the correct answer.

EXAMPLE

Adam applauded the diver as she stepped onto the podium to collect her Olympic silver medal.

In which sport did the athlete compete?

A   Rowing

B   Gymnastics

C   Hockey

(D)   Diving

E   Football

The following is an extract from 'Jack Russell Dog Breed' taken from www.petwave.com, an online source for pet owners

The Jack Russell Terrier, also sometimes called the Working Russell Terrier, the Working Jack Russell Terrier, the Jack and the JRT, is a lively little dog named after its originator, the Reverend John (Jack) Russell, an English man from the 19th century. Jack Russell Terriers were bred to accompany the hunt and go to ground to bolt fox. Ultimately, they were bred for temperament
5   and ability rather than consistency in type. An interesting fact about this breed is that a Jack Russell Terrier is the only dog ever to have set paws on both the North and the South Poles. Explorers Sir Ranulph Fiennes and his wife, Ginnie, apparently took their JRT, Bothie, on both of their transglobal expeditions from 1979 to 1982. Jack Russell Terriers are best known for their intense curiosity, extreme intelligence and endlessly entertaining personality. The Jack Russell
10   Terrier is not recognised by or eligible for registration with the English or American Kennel Clubs.

Jack Russell Terriers are the biggest dogs you'll ever meet in such a tiny package. They can run all day and keep coming back for more. They are sharply intelligent and absolutely nothing gets past them. There is no fooling a Jack Russell. They are spirited terriers, fearless and sassy with minds of their own and aren't above causing mischief to get a laugh. They are highly trainable
15   and are famous for their high-jumping antics. When raised alongside children, Jack Russells make fine family dogs. They are exceptional athletes who excel in the competitive arena.

Activity Requirements

Their size may make them appealing to apartment dwellers, but Jack Russells are not apartment dogs. Think of them as large dogs trapped in small bodies. They need lots of wide
20   open space to run and can feel cooped up inside a small apartment which will almost always lead to destructive behaviour. Fenced-in yards are a must, as Jack Russells will take off like a shot after cats, squirrels, rabbits, bikes and even cars. They should always be supervised when outdoors because these little guys love to dig and not only will they make quick work of a flower bed, but they will dig under fences to get out and seek new adventure.

25 Daily activities should include both walking and time to run in the yard. Jack Russells love to chase balls. They love it so much, in fact, that many owners believe their dogs are obsessed with playing ball. They will retrieve the ball as often as you are willing to throw it, and when you're done, they'll still want more.

Jack Russell Terriers are highly intelligent dogs and need as much mental stimulation as they
30 do physical activity. These dogs excel in agility activities and there are entire competitions set up around Jack Russell Terriers that include sprinting, flyball, obstacle courses and retrieving. Enrolling your Jack Russell in these types of activities ensures it's getting its daily physical and mental stimulation.

"Earth dog" activities, where dogs are allowed to dig in search of rodents, are also excellent
35 outlets for Jack Russells, as they satisfy their need to dig as well as their need to hunt. These activities are conducted with safety in mind, and the rodents are kept in safe enclosures, so that the dogs can't actually get to them.

Trainability

Jack Russells are highly trainable dogs and soak up new tasks like a sponge. They are terriers
40 and can exhibit stubbornness if they don't like the attitude of the person training them. Positive reinforcement and mixing up the daily training routine will keep your Jack Russell engaged and interested. Discipline and harsh tones will cause this dog to become defensive which may lead to snapping or biting.

Once basic obedience is mastered, Jack Russells should move on to advanced obedience, trick
45 training and agility work. They thrive on new activity and will be at the top of their class in just about every activity they participate in.

Behavioural Traits

Jack Russells are terriers, and they exhibit many classic terrier traits including excessive barking, wilfulness, rudeness to strangers, dog aggression, possessiveness and jealousy. Proper
50 training and socialisation from an early age can ensure an even-tempered dog.

Jacks should never be trusted off leash. They will take off like a shot after small animals and it is next to impossible to call them off.

Digging is a common complaint among Jack Russell owners. Turn your back on these guys for one second, and they can be halfway to the centre of the earth. Keeping an eye on your dog at all times
55 is important to keep your landscaping intact and to ensure your Jack doesn't escape under the fence.

① Who is the Jack Russell Terrier named after?

A A famous artist named Jack.

B An American reverend named Jack.

C A renowned dog breeder named Jack.

D A notorious criminal named Jack.

E None of the above.

② Which of the following characteristics are Jack Russells not known for?

A Inquisitiveness

B Cleverness

C Idleness

D A fondness for digging

E A fondness for chasing balls

Questions continue on next page

3 How will a Jack Russell Terrier react to being left in a small apartment?

A The Jack Russell will wait patiently.

B The Jack Russell will fall asleep.

C The Jack Russell will behave destructively.

D The Jack Russell will feel at ease.

E The Jack Russell will behave respectfully.

4 Why is taking part in an 'Earth dog' activity beneficial for a Jack Russell?

A It satisfies their need to hunt and eat rodents.

B It satisfies their need to swim.

C It satisfies their need to sharpen their claws.

D It satisfies their need to bark.

E It satisfies their need to dig.

5 According to the passage, which of the following helps to maintain the interest of a Jack Russell?

A Strict discipline

B Praise and rewards

C A comfortable new bed

D A severe tone of voice

E A repetitive routine

6 Which of the following is important in ensuring that a Jack Russell is good-tempered?

A Contact from an early age with humans and other dogs.

B A private space that they can call their own.

C The ability to roam freely with no restraints.

D The freedom to dig as and when they please.

E None of the above.

7 Why might it be dangerous to walk a Jack Russell on the street without a leash?

A The Jack Russell will attack all humans that pass by.

B The Jack Russell requires a leash in order to breathe.

C The Jack Russell might choke on the leash.

D The Jack Russell is easily distracted and could run into oncoming traffic.

E The Jack Russell is an easy target for larger dogs to attack.

8 Which of these words best describes the tone of this passage?

A Abrasive

B Fiction

C Imaginative

D Emotional

E Objective

9 What is the meaning of the word 'retrieve' as it is used in the passage? (line 27)

A Believe

B Fetch

C Attack

D Chase

E Ignore

10 What type of word is 'walking'? (line 25)

A Pronoun

B Adjective

C Noun

D Adverb

E Verb

Score: .... / 10

Spelling

You have 6 minutes to complete this test.

You have 12 questions to complete within the time given.

In each question, circle the letter below the group of words containing a spelling mistake.

If there is no mistake, circle the letter **N**.

EXAMPLE

The peeple at the festival enjoyed the party atmosphere as the moon rose high overhead.

    (A)   B   C   D   **N**

---

(1) The young students wanted to start an initiative to aid the beggers in the city.

    A   B   C   D   **N**

(2) The family anxiuosly awaited the news following the tribunal's deliberations.

    A   B   C   D   **N**

(3) The park rangers had forbbiden entry to all visitors until the issue was resolved.

    A   B   C   D   **N**

(4) The cheetah has escaped from her zoo enclosure and has so far aluded capture.

    A   B   C   D   **N**

(5) The thirsty pony could not wait to quench his thirst in the trough filled with cool water.

    A   B   C   D   **N**

Questions continue on next page

6. The royal delegation was accustomed to better treatment than it had been recieving.

    A   B   C   D   **N**

7. It's important to eat a holesome breakfast to provide you with sufficient energy.

    A   B   C   D   **N**

8. All of the properties were vaycated as the fire raged towards the centre of the town.

    A   B   C   D   **N**

9. "A prompt response would be most appreciated," requested the afflicted lady.

    A   B   C   D   **N**

10. The new plants flourished under the tender cultivation of the head gardener.

    A   B   C   D   **N**

11. The plumber had to remove the great to access the broken pipe running underneath.

    A   B   C   D   **N**

12. The child prodigy was able to resite Homer's Iliad from memory in the original Greek.

    A   B   C   D   **N**

Score: .... / 12

Punctuation

You have 6 minutes to complete this test.

You have 12 questions to complete within the time given.

In each question, circle the letter below the group of words containing a punctuation mistake.

If there is no mistake, circle the letter **N**.

EXAMPLE

The fireworks reflected in the thames to produce a brilliant and colourful display.
    A   (B)   C   D   N

(1) There were too many obstacles along the path so, unfortunately they had to turn back.
        A   B   C   D   N

(2) The City of London is divided into a number of different Regions known as boroughs.
        A   B   C   D   N

(3) There was only a little bit of time left when Henrietta cried, "Hurry up or we won't make it!"
        A   B   C   D   N

(4) After stirring the pot you need to add lemon, chillies and coriander and stir it all again.
        A   B   C   D   N

(5) There was a leak in the womens' changing room; they had to call a plumber to fix it.
        A   B   C   D   N

Questions continue on next page

6 Always remember to keep hold of the receipt, when making expensive purchases.

    A   B   C   D   **N**

7 Rita, who was in the process of moving house, was too busy to attend her friends' party.

    A   B   C   D   **N**

8 "Your request shouldnt cause any issues but I will need to double-check," said Julia.

    A   B   C   D   **N**

9 The conference will be held in our hotel (7th floor). Please sign in upon arrival.

    A   B   C   D   **N**

10 I work from Monday to Friday in May but only four days per week throughout Summer.

    A   B   C   D   **N**

11 "Diamonds are perceived as extremely valuable by many people" stated the jeweller.

    A   B   C   D   **N**

12 Mark slowly drank his coffee, finished his sweet pastry, and completed his crossword.

    A   B   C   D   **N**

Score: .... / 12

Sentence Completion

In each question, circle the letter below the word or group of words that most accurately completes the passage.

EXAMPLE

Finding a replacement | change | chart | chance | charge | charger | for her phone wasn't easy.
A   B   C   D   Ⓔ

---

1 The new statue was placed in the shop, | impressive | impressioning | impressing |
                                                    A   B   C

| impressed | | improvising | everyone that saw it.
       D   E

2 " | Wasn't | Were not | Was | Weren't | Werent | you supposed to arrive at
     A   B   C   D   E

midday?" asked Samantha.

3 Lucy was having so much fun that she forgot all | off | about | under | in | regarding |
                                                             A   B   C   D   E

her homework.

4 George was feeling a little | over | between | upon | forward | under | the weather so
                                            A   B   C   D   E

he decided to stay at home.

Questions continue on next page

(5) Alex liked to read his novel **whiling** **whole** **whilst** **meant** **during** aboard the
                                    A   B   C   D   E

train on the way to work.

(6) Though Fred was **generally** **general** **generalisation** **generalled** **generals**
                        A   B   C   D   E

happy with the performance, he had some criticisms.

(7) The blundering butcher had no one to blame **lest** **saved** **apart** **over** **but** himself
                        A   B   C   D   E

for his predicament.

(8) Deirdre had so far avoided **suspicious** **suspicion** **suspecting** **suspect** **suspend**
                    A   B   C   D   E

and was not of interest to the investigation.

(9) The boy **pled** **pleaded** **pleading** **pleased** **pleasant** with his father to buy him
            A   B   C   D   E

the new video game.

(10) The success of the project depended **in** **with** **on** **above** **for** a number of variable
                        A   B   C   D   E

factors.

(11) **Since** **Despite** **Moreover** **Furthermore** **Nevertheless** Peter was the first to
     A   B   C   D   E

arrive, he could choose whichever seat he liked.

(12) The rabid dogs were only kept **to** **up** **on** **at** **in** bay by the large steel fence.
                               A B C D E

Score: .... / 12

You have 10 minutes to complete this test.

You have 10 questions to complete within the time given.

Read the passage and answer the questions that follow. In each question, circle the letter next to the correct answer.

EXAMPLE

Adam applauded the diver as she stepped onto the podium to collect her Olympic silver medal.

In which sport did the athlete compete?

A   Rowing

B   Gymnastics

C   Hockey

D   Diving

E   Football

The following is an extract from 'Birds and your garden' by Natural England

Birds come to gardens to feed, breed, nest and rest. If water is provided, they will also visit to drink, bathe and preen their feathers. For a relatively small number of birds, gardens may supply most of their requirements for most of the year. More commonly, however, gardens offer a stopping-off point – somewhere to spend part of the day or night, or part of the year. Having
5   a greater appreciation of what birds need from gardens will enable you to provide for them to a greater degree.

Food

Although garden birds can be grouped artificially into broad categories such as insect-eaters and seed-eaters, the reality is less simple. Insectivores such as tits and woodpeckers also include
10   vegetable food in their diet and blackcaps are also very partial to winter fruits and berries. Correspondingly, in the first week or so of their lives, the nestlings of most seed-eating birds need the protein provided by insects and other invertebrates, such as spiders. The ideal garden for birds should therefore be able to supply both animal and vegetable food matter throughout the year. This has a number of practical implications.

15   The following is a list of tried and tested ways of ensuring a plentiful supply of invertebrate food for your birds:

• Maintain one or more compost heaps.

Passage continues on next page

- Keep dead wood, perhaps in a log pile.
- Allow leaves to rot down naturally rather than bagging and removing them in the autumn.
20 - Plant a wide variety of trees and shrubs, especially native species such as willow, oak and birch which support many caterpillars.
- Don't be obsessive about tidying away dead and dying perennials in the winter.
- Try developing at least part of your lawn as a wildflower meadow.

Most birds eat some vegetable matter and much is known about the preferred foods of
25 individual species. Goldfinches love the seeds of teasel, lavender and sunflower. Alder and silver birch trees may attract common redpolls if they are in the vicinity.

Starlings are fond of rowan berries and cherries, but will also eat the small black berries of Virginia creeper when really hungry. Bullfinches like the buds of forsythia and the seeds of forget-me-not.

30 Mistle thrushes don't just go for the berries of mistletoe from which they take their name: they will try and take possession of any fruiting holly or rowan tree and defend it fiercely from competitors.

Robins eat the attractive dual-coloured berries of the spindle tree, while ivy berries are a vital food source for blackcaps, blackbirds and wood pigeons, especially late in the year when there may be
35 little else available. Every gardener should try and make room for some apple trees: members of the thrush family, including winter visitors like redwing and fieldfare, will make short work of any windfalls.

Cats

Many gardens are visited by cats and it is important to help guard your birds against their
40 unwelcome attention. Position bird feeders and tables away from the low cover in which cats may hide and also provide perches nearby – vantage points from where birds can detect an approaching cat. Anecdotal evidence suggests that the more birds that visit a garden, the lower the chances of a cat being able to catch any one individual – probably because there are more pairs of eyes looking out for potential threats. If you are a cat owner, consider attaching a bell
45 or sonic bleeper to your cat to warn the local wildlife of its approach.

Drinking and bathing

All birds need to drink and to keep their feathers in good condition. Relatively few gardens offer birds safe drinking and bathing facilities so whatever you can do will help. If you can, dig a pond. Even very small water bodies can be excellent for wildlife but the pond should have shallow
50 edges so that birds can get to the water easily. Bird baths can be small or large, but a shallow dish shape is what's required – with a thin layer of gravel at the bottom if the material is liable to be slippery. Keep it unfrozen in cold weather.

Observations of garden birds by tens of thousands of people give organisations like the British Trust for Ornithology (BTO) invaluable information on trends in bird populations.

(1) Where would one most likely read this extract?

    A   In a biography of a renowned politician.

    B   In a sci-fi novel involving birds.

    C   On an advertising hoarding.

    D   In a leaflet at a shop selling birdfeed.

    E   In a book describing reptiles.

(2) What must be understood in order to provide for birds in a garden?

    A   The songs that birds sing in the morning.

    B   The various markings of different birds.

    C   The social rules of engagement with birds.

    D   The needs and requirements of birds.

    E   The hopes and dreams of birds.

(3) Why is it important that there are plenty of spiders and other invertebrates in the garden?

    A   Birds don't like to feast on insects.

    B   They help with air purification.

    C   They keep cats away from the garden.

    D   They provide nourishment for recently born birds.

    E   They make sure that birds are alerted to predators.

(4) Why are birds attracted to birch trees?

    A   Birch trees are ideal for nesting.

    B   Birch tree bark contains vital vitamins for birds.

    C   Birch trees aid with effective camouflage.

    D   Birch trees are home to suitable prey for birds.

    E   Birch trees are the most aesthetically pleasing to birds.

(5) Which of these statements is true?

    A   Cats always catch birds in groups.

    B   Birds always escape from predators when they are alone.

    C   Birds, when in groups, keep cats at bay.

    D   Cats don't like to catch individual birds.

    E   Birds are never hunted by cats.

Questions continue on next page

6 What should a cat owner do to help protect birds from attack?

    A   The cat should be kept indoors all the time.

    B   The cat should be trained not to hunt birds.

    C   The cat should be fed a vegetarian diet.

    D   The cat should be directed towards squirrels.

    E   The cat should be made less effective as a predator.

7 Which of the following would be a hindrance to birds?

    A   Small water bodies

    B   Bird feeders and tables

    C   Apple trees

    D   Wildflower meadows

    E   Deep bird baths

8 Which of these statements is not mentioned in the passage?

    A   Goldfinches are fond of sunflower seeds.

    B   Starlings are fond of cherries.

    C   Bullfinches are fond of forget-me-not seeds.

    D   Mistle thrushes are fond of rowan trees.

    E   Blackbirds are fond of apple trees.

9 What is the meaning of the word 'obsessive', as it is used in the passage? (line 22)

    A   Devotee

    B   Buff

    C   Fanatical

    D   Follower

    E   Admire

10 What type of word is 'preferred'? (line 24)

    A   Adjective

    B   Noun

    C   Verb

    D   Adverb

    E   Pronoun

Score: .... / 10

Spelling

You have 6 minutes to complete this test.

You have 12 questions to complete within the time given.

In each question, circle the letter below the group of words containing a spelling mistake.

If there is no mistake, circle the letter **N**.

EXAMPLE

The peeple at the festival enjoyed the party atmosphere as the moon rose high overhead.

  (A)   B   C   D   **N**

---

(1)   Most of the patience in the hospital were suffering from either diabetes or cancer.

  A   B   C   D   **N**

(2)   The bells pealed in the church, signalling that it was time for the Sunday service.

  A   B   C   D   **N**

(3)   The TV channel was inundated with complaints after heiring the controversial show.

  A   B   C   D   **N**

(4)   The circus owner was unwilling to put a holt to proceedings as it would cost him dearly.

  A   B   C   D   **N**

(5)   The scientist was unable to procure the required chemicals to conduct the experiment.

  A   B   C   D   **N**

Questions continue on next page

6 Jerry's reputation in the community was badly tarenished after his unprovoked outburst.

    A   B   C   D   **N**

7 The intern did not sease to badger his manager about the possibility of employment.

    A   B   C   D   **N**

8 The rhino submited to the hippopotamus's superior force and left the watering hole.

    A   B   C   D   **N**

9 Sheep are generally docile creatures with a calm, passive and gentle nature.

    A   B   C   D   **N**

10 I was warry of getting involved with the cause as I had been advised to avoid it.

    A   B   C   D   **N**

11 Ian was reluctant to abandon the campain but his odds were looking increasingly slim.

    A   B   C   D   **N**

12 The aggressive and poisonuos hornets were whipped into a fearful frenzy by the attack.

    A   B   C   D   **N**

Questions continue on next page

Score: .... / 12

You have **6 minutes** to complete this test.

You have **12 questions** to complete within the time given.

In each question, circle the letter below the group of words containing a punctuation mistake.

If there is no mistake, circle the letter **N**.

EXAMPLE

The fireworks reflected in the thames to produce a brilliant and colourful display.

    A   Ⓑ   C   D   N

---

(1) There weren't many choices available I think we should go to the other restaurant.

    A   B   C   D   N

(2) Relieved that she had not been caught Rebecca quietly crept out of the basement.

    A   B   C   D   N

(3) The young man won't help you. He isnt interested in being a part of your charade.

    A   B   C   D   N

(4) The new doctor, who had just arrived from Holland was known to be highly skilled.

    A   B   C   D   N

(5) "We will all gather this evening to discuss all our issues and grievances", said Martha.

    A   B   C   D   N

Questions continue on next page

6 Sven didn't believe in ghosts. Furthermore he thought those who did were foolish.

A   B   C   D   **N**

7 The tourists were keen to visit the Village as it was known to be very picturesque.

A   B   C   D   **N**

8 We couldn't believe that there were no more petrol stations en route until birmingham.

A   B   C   D   **N**

9 My bags' did not arrive on the belt. Furthermore, the handlers were unable to find them.

A   B   C   D   **N**

10 When we go to the beach we like to pack sandwiches and snacks to eat by the sea.

A   B   C   D   **N**

11 We mustn't forget to try all the rides: The Sizzler, The Draculator and The Rollerball.

A   B   C   D   **N**

12 Little by little, the foundations of the ancient monument were slowly crumbling.

A   B   C   D   **N**

Score: .... / 12

Sentence Completion

In each question, circle the letter below the word or group of words that most accurately completes the passage.

EXAMPLE

Finding a replacement | change | chart | chance | charge | charger | for her phone wasn't easy.
                         A   B   C   D   Ⓔ

1. All the children were looking forward to dressing | in | on | over | below | up | in
                                                         A   B   C   D   E

   their costumes.

2. "| Whomever | Whatsoever | Whichever | Whoever | Whenever | finds the ring can
        A   B   C   D   E

   keep it!" declared the magnanimous ruler.

3. Tess decided to give her friend the benefit | in | upon | of | through | for | the doubt in
                                                   A   B   C   D   E

   this instance.

4. Jason | read | looked | heard | wrote | bowled | out of the window and saw a bird
            A   B   C   D   E

   soaring through the sky.

Questions continue on next page

(5) We could not decide | **weather** | **whatsoever** | **whether** | **wetter** | **whoever** | to paint
                     A   **B**   **C**   **D**   **E**

the wall green, blue or red.

(6) | **Believing** | **Believed** | **Believer** | **Belief** | **Belie** | that he had won the game, Dan
    A   **B**   **C**   **D**   **E**

triumphantly burst into the room.

(7) Michelle's parents could only guess | **of** | **in** | **on** | **for** | **as** | to why she was so upset.
                              A **B** **C** **D** **E**

(8) Aunt Petra asked me to turn | **up** | **down** | **back** | **lower** | **decrease** | the volume as it
                        A   **B**   **C**   **D**   **E**

was too loud.

(9) The heedless gazelles were unaware of the | **pride** | **shoal** | **herd** | **troop** | **school** | of
                                     A   **B**   **C**   **D**   **E**

lions creeping up on them.

(10) The brave fireman persisted | **in** | **for** | **on** | **when** | **by** | his efforts to save the stranded
                              A **B** **C**   **D**   **E**

civilians.

(11) Linda | **was run** | **had been run** | **had been running** | **has been running** | **runs** | for
           A   **B**   **C**   **D**   **E**

two months when she decided to enter the race.

(12) The team's weary fans hoped | **about** | **in** | **by** | **how** | **for** | some positive news regarding
                            A   **B** **C**   **D** **E**

transfers.

Score: .... / 12

Comprehension

Read the passage and answer the questions that follow. In each question, circle the letter next to the correct answer.

EXAMPLE

Adam applauded the diver as she stepped onto the podium to collect her Olympic silver medal.

In which sport did the athlete compete?

A   Rowing

B   Gymnastics

C   Hockey

(D)   Diving

E   Football

The following is an extract from 'The Little Princess' by Frances Hodgson Burnett

On that first morning, when Sara sat at Miss Minchin's side, aware that the whole schoolroom was devoting itself to observing her, she had noticed very soon one little girl, about her own age, who looked at her very hard with a pair of light, rather dull, blue eyes. She was a fat child who did not look as if she were in the least clever, but she had a good-naturedly pouting mouth. Her
5 flaxen hair was braided in a tight pigtail, tied with a ribbon, and she had pulled this pigtail around her neck, and was biting the end of the ribbon, resting her elbows on the desk, as she stared wonderingly at the new pupil. When Monsieur Dufarge began to speak to Sara, she looked a little frightened; and when Sara stepped forward and, looking at him with the innocent, appealing eyes, answered him, without any warning, in French, the fat little girl gave a startled jump, and
10 grew quite red in her awed amazement. Having wept hopeless tears for weeks in her efforts to remember that "la mère" meant "the mother", and "le père", "the father",— when one spoke sensible English — it was almost too much for her suddenly to find herself listening to a child her own age who seemed not only quite familiar with these words, but apparently knew any number of others, and could mix them up with verbs as if they were mere trifles.

15 She stared so hard and bit the ribbon on her pigtail so fast that she attracted the attention of Miss Minchin, who, feeling extremely cross at the moment, immediately pounced upon her.

"Miss St. John!" she exclaimed severely. "What do you mean by such conduct? Remove your elbows! Take your ribbon out of your mouth! Sit up at once!"

Passage continues on next page

Upon which Miss St. John gave another jump, and when Lavinia and Jessie giggled she became
20 redder than ever — so red, indeed, that she almost looked as if tears were coming into her
poor, dull, childish eyes; and Sara saw her and was so sorry for her that she began rather to
like her and want to be her friend. It was a way of hers always to want to spring into any fray
in which someone was made uncomfortable or unhappy.

"If Sara had been a boy and lived a few centuries ago," her father used to say, "she would have
25 gone about the country with her sword drawn, rescuing and defending everyone in distress. She
always wants to fight when she sees people in trouble."

So she took rather a fancy to fat, slow, little Miss St. John, and kept glancing toward her
through the morning. She saw that lessons were no easy matter to her, and that there was
no danger of her ever being spoiled by being treated as a show pupil. Her French lesson was
30 a pathetic thing. Her pronunciation made even Monsieur Dufarge smile in spite of himself, and
Lavinia and Jessie and the more fortunate girls either giggled or looked at her in wondering
scorn. But Sara did not laugh. She tried to look as if she did not hear when Miss St. John called
"le bon pain", "lee bong pang". She had a fine, hot little temper of her own, and it made her feel
rather savage when she heard the titters and saw the poor, stupid, distressed child's face.

① Where is this passage set?

A   In a hotel

B   In a church

C   In a school

D   In a park

E   In a student's home

② Who had 'rather dull, blue eyes'?

A   Sara

B   Miss Minchin

C   Monsieur Dufarge

D   Lavinia

E   Miss St. John

③ Who had blonde hair?

A   Miss St. John

B   Sara

C   Jessie

D   Lavinia

E   Miss Minchin

④ Why do you think Miss St. John bit her ribbon?

A   The ribbon tasted good.

B   She thought it would amuse the rest of the pupils.

C   She felt amazed and uneasy.

D   She was a very bright student.

E   She liked eating ribbons.

(5) Why was Sara a little frightened initially?

A It was her first day in an unfamiliar environment.

B She had not finished her homework.

C Her teacher was mean.

D She couldn't understand French.

E The other girls were rude towards her.

(6) What surprised Miss St. John?

A Sara's conceit and superiority in class

B Sara's modesty

C Sara's fluency in French

D Sara's arrogance and vanity

E Sara's indifferent nature

(7) How did the girls, other than Sara, behave towards Miss St. John?

A They ridiculed her.

B They tried to help her in overcoming her fear of learning.

C They were very sympathetic and supportive.

D They didn't bother her at all.

E They were considerate and caring.

(8) What can be inferred about Sara's personality?

A She was indifferent and cold.

B She was protective of those in distress.

C She was proud and vain.

D She was high-handed and bossy.

E She showed no empathy to people around her.

(9) What is the meaning of 'pathetic', as it is used in the passage? (line 30)

A Unimpressive

B Strong

C Robust

D Resilient

E Persuasive

(10) What type of word is 'scorn'? (line 32)

A Verb

B Adverb

C Adjective

D Noun

E Pronoun

Score: .... / 10

<table>
<tr><td rowspan="2">Test
26</td><td colspan="2"># Spelling</td></tr>
</table>

In each question, circle the letter below the group of words containing a spelling mistake.

If there is no mistake, circle the letter N.

EXAMPLE

The peeple at the festival enjoyed the party atmosphere as the moon rose high overhead.

    (A)   B   C   D   **N**

(1) The bank manager was encouraged to offer more lones to her customers.

    A   B   C   D   **N**

(2) The inspectors were baffled as to how the scarcely beleivable theft had occurred.

    A   B   C   D   **N**

(3) "We need five more volounteers," demanded Mrs Wood in the school assembly.

    A   B   C   D   **N**

(4) The ekologist had devoted her life to the protection of rainforest habitats for apes.

    A   B   C   D   **N**

(5) The rain pored down on to the mountain, causing a landslide that wrecked the village.

    A   B   C   D   **N**

(6) All of the soldiers perished when they were outflanked by the opposing force.

    A   B   C   D   **N**

(7) To the disbelief of the court, the king ruled that the traitor be pardoned and set free.

    A   **B**   **C**   **D**   **N**

(8) Many people are against the proposal to use animal fur in our clothing and accessories.

    A   **B**   **C**   **D**   **N**

(9) The coach questioned the committment of his players during his halftime team talk.

    A   **B**   **C**   **D**   **N**

(10) A new ventilation shaft must be added to the building, according to new regulations.

    A   **B**   **C**   **D**   **N**

(11) Jim often talked allowed to himself when alone as it helped him to clear his thoughts.

    A   **B**   **C**   **D**   **N**

(12) The forgetfull man wandered out of the supermarket, neglecting to pay for his groceries.

    A   **B**   **C**   **D**   **N**

Score. .... / 12

In each question, circle the letter below the group of words containing a punctuation mistake.

If there is no mistake, circle the letter **N**.

EXAMPLE

The fireworks reflected in the thames to produce a brilliant and colourful display.

A   (B)   C   D   N

① The raindrops did not stop falling; A small puddle began to form at Vincent's doorstep.

A   B   C   D   N

② The chef quickly whipped up some delicious, poached eggs for the famished guests.

A   B   C   D   N

③ "Shouldn't you be at school at this time of day?" Demanded the suspicious shopkeeper.

A   B   C   D   N

④ The new station – built at a cost of £50 million – contained state-of-the-art technology.

A   B   C   D   N

⑤ The large green tractor was Ben's pride and joy. He polished it thoroughly every morning.

A   B   C   D   N

⑥ Feeling weak after the day's events, Janette decided to take a warm bath in the evening.

A   B   C   D   N

7 There were many new paintings in the gallery for the interested buyers to peruse.

    A   B   C   D   **N**

8 "The plane will need to make an emergency landing. Brace! Brace!" declared the pilot

    A   B   C   D   **N**

9 "You must keep going," declared the instructor. "You are very close to the end".

    A   B   C   D   **N**

10 The queen's new palace will be built on the north bank of the winding river.

    A   B   C   D   **N**

11 The cost of a loaf of bread has increased dramatically by %50 over the last 4 weeks.

    A   B   C   D   **N**

12 Mr Trotter was an excellent teacher whom the students listened to attentively.

    A   B   C   D   **N**

Score: / 12

Sentence Completion

You have 6 minutes to complete this test.

You have 12 questions to complete within the time given.

In each question, circle the letter below the word or group of words that most accurately completes the passage.

EXAMPLE

Finding a replacement | **change** | **chart** | **chance** | **charge** | **charger** | for her phone wasn't easy.
                      A   B   C   D   Ⓔ

① "That would be the | **more worse** | **worser** | **worst** | **worstest** | **most bad** | possible
                        A   B   C   D   E

outcome," agreed Mr Summers.

② The criminal confessed | **of** | **from** | **about** | **with** | **to** | the crime in the hope of receiving a
                     A   B   C   D   E

lighter sentence.

③ "Actions speak | **louder** | **loudest** | **loud** | **lout** | **prouder** | than words," stated the
               A   B   C   D   E

engineer pompously.

④ Rachel could choose | **whether** | **whomever** | **whatever** | **whichever** | **whatsoever** |
                      A   B   C   D   E

she liked as a partner for the project.

⑤ | **On** | **For** | **In** | **Above** | **Towards** | conclusion, the committee decided to suggest a raft
  A   B   C   D   E

of changes.

(6) The tree | **weathered** | **blossomed** | **sprung** | **withered** | **grew** | away and died in the
              A   **B**   **C**   **D**   **E**

harsh winter.

(7) "I am not keen to go | **and** | **but** | **so** | **furthermore** | **since** | I will if you want me to,"
                     A   **B**   **C**   **D**   **E**

said Richard.

(8) Both | **teacher's** | **teachers** | **teacher** | **teaches** | **teachers'** | classes contained
         A   **B**   **C**   **D**   **E**

thirty pupils.

(9) It is certainly not easy to | **mastering** | **mastered** | **master** | **masterer** | **mast** | the art
                          A   **B**   **C**   **D**   **E**

of wine tasting.

(10) Ingrid was deterred | **from** | **to** | **in** | **with** | **about** | pursuing the matter by her friends and
                    A   **B** **C**   **D**   **E**

family.

(11) Jade had lost so much weight that Leo mistook her | **about** | **for** | **regarding** | **as in** | **like**
                                          A   **B**   **C**   **D**   **E**

someone else.

(12) Upon | **received** | **receptive** | **receival** | **receipt** | **receiving** | of his degree, Charles
              A   **B**   **C**   **D**   **E**

began to look for a job in the countryside.

Score: / 12

Spelling

You have 6 minutes to complete this test.

You have 12 questions to complete within the time given.

In each question, circle the letter below the group of words containing a spelling mistake.

If there is no mistake, circle the letter **N**.

EXAMPLE

The peeple at the festival enjoyed the party atmosphere as the moon rose high overhead.

Ⓐ   B   C   D   N

① The girl let out a large grown when she learned that she would have to babysit her sister.

A   B   C   D   N

② The delicate glass sculptures were wrapped in a protective layer of foam and cardboard.

A   B   C   D   N

③ The ernest young man impressed almost everyone who came into contact with him.

A   B   C   D   N

④ There are many famous fables that highlite the quick wit and cunning of foxes.

A   B   C   D   N

⑤ "We must try and find an economical solution!" demanded the stressed bussinesman.

A   B   C   D   N

⑥ Poorly trained soldiers will often flea the battlefield at the first sign of trouble.

A   B   C   D   N

(7) The bewildered nurse was thrust into the limelight and was quite unsure how to react.

A   B   C   D   N

(8) Rowbust plans and quality materials are the key to the success of construction projects.

A   B   C   D   N

(9) Both Linda and Faisal eyed the last peace of the delicious chocolate cake ravenously.

A   B   C   D   N

(10) The unlucky parents were lieable for all the damage caused by their unruly child.

A   B   C   D   N

(11) The surface of a shark's skin is rough and course to the touch, similar to sandpaper.

A   B   C   D   N

(12) Lots of pedestrians sneaked admiring and jealous glances at her sleak new sports car.

A   B   C   D   N

Notes

Answers

Test 1 Comprehension

Q1 **C** *Three*
The narrator, Merrylegs and the mare.

Q2 **B** *May*
'It was early in May…'

Q3 **C** *Squire Gordon*
'It was early in May, when there came a man from Squire Gordon's, who took me away to the hall.'

Q4 **B** *It was very spacious and airy.*
'…this was very roomy, with four good stalls; a large swinging window opened into the yard, which made it pleasant and airy.'

Q5 **B** *It is a stall in which the horse is not tied up.*
'…it was called a loose box, because the horse that was put into it was not tied up, but left loose, to do as he liked.'

Q6 **E** *The horse was very happy to leave his first master and move to the new stable.*
There is no evidence to suggest this.

Q7 **A** *Pretty and plump, with a thick mane and tail.*
'In the stall next to mine stood a little fat gray horse, with a thick mane and tail, a very pretty head, and a pert little nose.'

Q8 **A** *Because she had to vacate her stall to make room for the new horse.*
"So it is you who have turned me out of my box; it is a very strange thing for a colt like you to come and turn a lady out of her own home."

Q9 **C** *Tied*

Q10 **D** *Verbs*

Test 2 Spelling

Q1 **C** *dependable*

Q2 **A** *assistants*

Q3 **C** *according*

Q4 **A** *cooperation*

Q5 **N**

Q6 **D** *decency*

Q7 **A** *stationery*

Q8 **B** *essential*

Q9 **N**

Q10 **C** *vial*

Q11 **B** *steal*

Q12 **C** *transferred*

Test 3 Punctuation

Q1 **B** *London*

Q2 **D** *infection.*

Q3 **N**

Q4 **A** *Ben, James*

Q5 **A** *going?"*

Q6 **A** *isn't*

Q7 **N**

Q8 **C** *However, she*

Q9 **B** *ingredients: butter*

Q10 **C** *pause; many* **OR** *pause. Many*

Q11 **B** *meat and*

Q12 **D** *Rebecca*

Test 4 Sentence Completion

Q1 **C** *them*

Q2 **A** *past*

Q3 **C** *at*

Q4 **E** *whole*

Q5 **C** *Despite*

Q6 **D** *could have*

Q7 **B** *who*

Q8 **B** *Stay*

Q9 **C** *through*

Q10 **A** *be*

Q11 **C** *However*

Q12 **B** *has been going*

Test 5 Comprehension

Q1 **C** *Avoid the Cyclops.*
'…and generally worth going a long way to avoid.'

Q2 **D** *Cyclopes were incredibly dim-witted.*
'…the Cyclops was also incredibly stupid.'

Q3 **B** *Their memory and understanding were poor.*
'…the Cyclopes were poor conversationalists, often forgetting the beginning of a sentence when they were only halfway through.'

Q4 **E** *He cherished his close relationship with them.*
'Polyphemus had no friends but was on intimate terms with most of the sheep.'

Test 5 answers continue on next page

Q5 **A** *In a cave*

'One day, returning to his cave after a hard day's work...'

Q6 **B** *He was overjoyed.*

'...he was delighted to see that they were human beings.'

Q7 **A** *The men gathered together in fright.*

'The men had by now huddled together and were looking up at him with a mixture of horror and terror.'

Q8 **D** *The men were in search of food and water.*

"We stopped here to find fresh provisions for our ship..."

Q9 **A** *Generosity*

Q10 **D** *Peaceful*

Test 6 Spelling

Q1 **A** *climbers*

Q2 **D** *incredible*

Q3 **N**

Q4 **B** *extremely*

Q5 **B** *guest*

Q6 **D** *practice*

Q7 **C** *occasion*

Q8 **B** *agreeable*

Q9 **B** *ledger*

Q10 **A** *wandered*

Q11 **B** *breath*

Q12 **B** *exercise*

Test 7 Punctuation

Q1 **B** *that?"*

Q2 **C** *course, a*

Q3 **D** *Nevertheless, we*

Q4 **N**

Q5 **D** *film: Star Wars.* **OR** *film, Star Wars.* **OR** *film - Star Wars.*

Q6 **B** *north*

Q7 **A** *weren't*

Q8 **C** *The Codfather*

Q9 **C** *harm,"*

Q10 **D** *decade.*

Q11 **N**

Q12 **B** *shoppers, Vikki*

Test 8 Sentence Completion

Q1 **B** *to*

Q2 **B** *There's*

Q3 **B** *was*

Q4 **D** *comparatively*

Q5 **A** *on*

Q6 **E** *you're*

Q7 **C** *that*

Q8 **C** *over*

Q9 **B** *see*

Q10 **D** *of*

Q11 **E** *from*

Q12 **E** *need*

Test 9 Comprehension

Q1 **C** *April*

'When I left my office that beautiful spring day...'

Q2 **C** *He was relaxed and content.*

'It was one of those days when a man feels good...'

Q3 **B** *It would be cleared by the sanitation department.*

'...the sanitation department would have to pick up a dead dog.'

Q4 **A** *The narrator had been saved by a dog.*

According to the quoted sentence, a dog had given his life to save the man.

Q5 **A** *He swung his coat at them.*

'My yelling and scolding didn't have much effect, but the swinging coat did.'

Q6 **E** *The hound was at first on guard but then approached the man.*

'The fighting fire slowly left his eyes...On his stomach, an inch at a time, he came to me and laid his head in my hand.'

Q7 **E** *His skin was stretched drum-tight over his bony frame.*

The quote indicates that he was very thin as a result of starvation.

Q8 **D** *The old hound belonged to the local neighbourhood.*

'I knew he had come a long way...'

Q9 **C** *The narrator was surprised.*

Q10 **E** *Examination*

Test 10 Spelling

Q1 **B** *capacity*

Q2 **B** *arguments*

Q3 **A** *ought*

Q4   **C**   *effects*

Q5   **N**

Q6   **N**

Q7   **B**   *buried*

Q8   **C**   *cupboard*

Q9   **D**   *aisle*

Q10   **C**   *inventors*

Q11   **B**   *bred*

Q12   **A**   *apartment*

Test 11 Punctuation

Q1   **B**   *lights*

Q2   **B**   *life?*

Q3   **D**   *its*

Q4   **B**   *autumn*

Q5   **N**

Q6   **D**   *and sand*

Q7   **B**   *seven, the*

Q8   **B**   *Thursday*

Q9   **C**   *referee. "Please*

Q10   **N**

Q11   **D**   *o'clock*

Q12   **C**   *fight, Daisy*

Test 12 Sentence Completion

Q1   **D**   *animals*

Q2   **C**   *ate*

Q3   **D**   *in*

Q4   **A**   *which*

Q5   **C**   *were*

Q6   **B**   *her*

Q7   **D**   *than*

Q8   **C**   *quickly*

Q9   **E**   *as*

Q10   **A**   *Don't*

Q11   **D**   *Get*

Q12   **C**   *in*

Test 13 Comprehension

Q1   **C**   *To change the reader's outlook towards the countryside.*

'This article is an endeavour to change the attitude of people towards the countryside.'

Q2   **B**   *Storms have driven them inland.*

'…seagulls, buffeted inland by the storm…'

Q3   **B**   *It has remained the same.*

'But the lane remains unchanged.'

Q4   **E**   *Wet and soggy land*

'It is always damp. It's where the ferns flourish…'

Q5   **C**   *Birds' nests*

'There are treasures in a Devon hedgerow…like birds' nests…'

Q6   **B**   *The river*

'The river is a silver ribbon; beside it parallel silver threads show the route of the railway…'

Q7   **A**   *The author is shielded from urban life by the countryside.*

The author feels like she is in a cocoon in the countryside that shields her from the local urban centre, Exeter.

Q8   **D**   *The country lane*

'…I soak up the tranquillity of a Devon lane – the ultimate rural icon.'

Q9   **B**   *Metaphor*

Q10   **D**   *Noun*

Test 14 Spelling

Q1   **A**   *surveyed*

Q2   **C**   *sturdy*

Q3   **C**   *dough*

Q4   **N**

Q5   **D**   *atmosphere*

Q6   **C**   *installations*

Q7   **B**   *pair*

Q8   **C**   *grateful*

Q9   **A**   *secretary*

Q10   **B**   *accept*

Q11   **C**   *eager*

Q12   **C**   *unfair*

Test 15 Punctuation

Q1   **A**   *"What's*

Q2   **B**   *fish: tuna,*

Q3   **D**   *its*

Q4   **D**   *wailed*

Q5   **C**   *ugly, heavy*

Q6   **N**

Q7   **C**   *grass, follow*

Test 15 answers continue on next page

Q8   D   *soon."*
Q9   N
Q10 N
Q11 N
Q12 B   *bank*

Test 16 Sentence Completion

Q1   B   *become*
Q2   C   *of*
Q3   A   *to*
Q4   B   *have failed*
Q5   D   *Whichever*
Q6   B   *strong*
Q7   D   *However*
Q8   B   *put*
Q9   E   *so*
Q10 E   *Whereas*
Q11 A   *lazily*
Q12 E   *off*

Test 17 Comprehension

Q1   E   *None of the above.*
         '…named after its originator, the Reverend John (Jack) Russell, an English man…'

Q2   C   *Idleness*
         'They can run all day and keep coming back for more.'

Q3   C   *The Jack Russell will behave destructively.*
         '…can feel cooped up inside a small apartment which will almost always lead to destructive behaviour.'

Q4   E   *It satisfies their need to dig.*
         '…it satisfies their need to dig…'

Q5   B   *Praise and rewards*
         'Positive reinforcement and mixing up the daily training routine will keep your Jack Russell engaged and interested.'

Q6   A   *Contact from an early age with humans and other dogs.*
         'Proper training and socialisation from an early age can ensure an even-tempered dog.'

Q7   D   *The Jack Russell is easily distracted and could run into oncoming traffic.*
         'They will take off like a shot after small animals and it is next to impossible to call them off.'

Q8   E   *Objective*
         The passage offers a balanced view of the possible positive and negative characteristics of a Jack Russell.

Q9   B   *Fetch*
Q10 C   *Noun*

Test 18 Spelling

Q1   D   *beggars*
Q2   A   *anxiously*
Q3   B   *forbidden*
Q4   D   *eluded*
Q5   N
Q6   D   *receiving*
Q7   B   *wholesome*
Q8   B   *vacated*
Q9   N
Q10 N
Q11 C   *grate*
Q12 C   *recite*

Test 19 Punctuation

Q1   C   *so, unfortunately, they* **OR** *path, so unfortunately* **OR** *so unfortunately they*
Q2   C   *regions*
Q3   N
Q4   B   *pot,*
Q5   B   *women's*
Q6   C   *receipt when*
Q7   N
Q8   A   *shouldn't*
Q9   N
Q10 D   *summer*
Q11 C   *people,"*
Q12 C   *pastry and*

Test 20 Sentence Completion

Q1   C   *impressing*
Q2   D   *Weren't*
Q3   B   *about*
Q4   E   *under*
Q5   C   *whilst*
Q6   A   *generally*
Q7   E   *but*

Q8	B	suspicion
Q9	B	pleaded
Q10	C	on
Q11	A	Since
Q12	D	at

Test 21 Comprehension

Q1	D	In a leaflet at a shop selling birdfeed.

The extract is factual and provides information about birds and how to cater for them in your garden.

Q2	D	The needs and requirements of birds.

'Having a greater appreciation of what birds need from gardens will enable you to provide for them to a greater degree.'

Q3	D	They provide nourishment for recently born birds.

'Correspondingly, in the first week or so of their lives, the nestlings of most seed-eating birds need the protein provided by insects and other invertebrates, such as spiders.'

Q4	D	Birch trees are home to suitable prey for birds.

'…and birch which support many caterpillars.'

Q5	C	Birds, when in groups, keep cats at bay.

'Anecdotal evidence suggests that the more birds that visit a garden, the lower the chances of a cat being able to catch any one individual…'

Q6	E	The cat should be made less effective as a predator.

'If you are a cat owner, consider attaching a bell or sonic bleeper to your cat to warn the local wildlife of its approach.'

Q7	E	Deep bird baths

'Bird baths can be small or large, but a shallow dish shape is what's required…'

Q8	E	Blackbirds are fond of apple trees.

This is not stated in the passage.

Q9	C	Fanatical
Q10	A	Adjective

Test 22 Spelling

Q1	A	patients
Q2	N	
Q3	D	airing
Q4	C	halt
Q5	N	
Q6	C	tarnished
Q7	B	cease
Q8	A	submitted
Q9	N	

Q10	A	wary
Q11	B	campaign
Q12	B	poisonous

Test 23 Punctuation

Q1	B	available. I **OR** available; I **OR** available - I
Q2	C	caught, Rebecca
Q3	C	isn't
Q4	C	Holland, was
Q5	D	grievances,"
Q6	B	Furthermore, he
Q7	B	village
Q8	D	Birmingham
Q9	A	bags
Q10	B	beach, we
Q11	N	
Q12	N	

Test 24 Sentence Completion

Q1	E	up
Q2	D	Whoever
Q3	C	of
Q4	B	looked
Q5	C	whether
Q6	A	Believing
Q7	E	as
Q8	B	down
Q9	A	pride
Q10	A	in
Q11	C	had been running
Q12	E	for

Test 25 Comprehension

Q1	C	In a school

'…the whole schoolroom…'

Q2	E	Miss St. John

'…one little girl, about her own age, who looked at her very hard with a pair of light, rather dull, blue eyes.'

Q3	A	Miss St. John

'Her flaxen hair was braided…'

Test 25 answers continue on next page

Q4 C She felt amazed and uneasy.

She felt insecure about Sara's proficiency in French. '…when Sara stepped forward and, looking at him with the innocent, appealing eyes, answered him, without any warning, in French, the fat little girl gave a startled jump, and grew quite red in her awed amazement.'

Q5 A It was her first day in an unfamiliar environment.

'On that first morning…aware that the whole schoolroom was devoting itself to observing her.'

Q6 C Sara's fluency in French

'…it was almost too much for her suddenly to find herself listening to a child her own age who seemed not only quite familiar with these words, but apparently knew any number of others, and could mix them up with verbs as if they were mere trifles.'

Q7 A They ridiculed her.

'…Lavinia and Jessie and the more fortunate girls either giggled or looked at her in wondering scorn.'

Q8 B She was protective of those in distress.

'It was a way of hers always to want to spring into any fray in which someone was made uncomfortable or unhappy.'

Q9 A Unimpressive

Q10 D Noun

Test 26 Spelling

Q1 C loans

Q2 C believable

Q3 B volunteers

Q4 A ecologist

Q5 A poured

Q6 N

Q7 N

Q8 N

Q9 B commitment

Q10 N

Q11 B aloud

Q12 A forgetful

Test 27 Punctuation

Q1 B falling; a **OR** falling. A

Q2 B delicious poached

Q3 C day?" demanded

Q4 N

Q5 N

Q6 N

Q7 N

Q8 D pilot.

Q9 D end."

Q10 N

Q11 D 50%

Q12 N

Test 28 Sentence Completion

Q1 C worst

Q2 E to

Q3 A louder

Q4 B whomever

Q5 C In

Q6 D withered

Q7 B but

Q8 E teachers'

Q9 C master

Q10 A from

Q11 B for

Q12 D receipt

Test 29 Spelling

Q1 B groan

Q2 N

Q3 A earnest

Q4 C highlight

Q5 D businessman

Q6 B flee

Q7 N

Q8 A Robust

Q9 B piece

Q10 B liable

Q11 C coarse

Q12 D sleek